Young Heroes

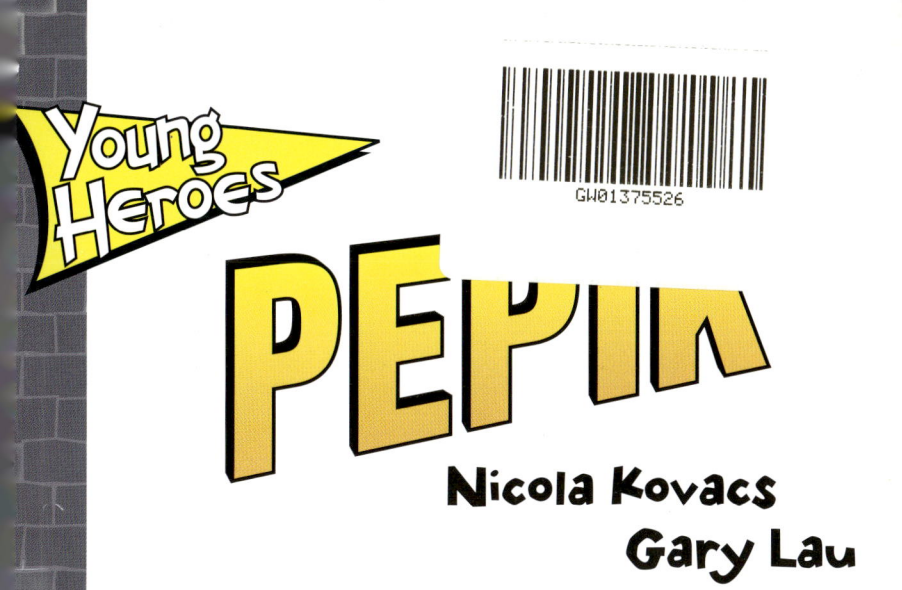

PEPIK

Nicola Kovacs
Gary Lau

RISING ★ STARS

For Heather, Elizabeth and Tomas.

First published in the UK by
Rising Stars UK Ltd.
7 Hatchers Mews, Bermondsey Street, London SE1 3GS
www.risingstars-uk.com

This edition published 2011

Text © UC Publishing Pty Ltd.
www.ucpublishing.com

First published 2006 by Insight Publications Pty Ltd.
ABN 57 005 102 983,
89 Wellington Street,
St Kilda, Victoria 3182
Australia

Development: UC Publishing Pty Ltd
Cover design: UC Publishing/Design Ed
Written by: Nicola Kovacs
Illustrations: Gary Lau
Text design and typesetting: Design Ed/Clive Sutherland
Editorial consultancy: Dee Reid

All rights reserved. No part of this publication may be reproduced, stored in a retrieval system or transmitted in any form by any means, electronic, mechanical, photocopying, recording or otherwise without the prior permission of Rising Stars Ltd.

British Library Cataloguing in Publication Data.
A CIP record for this book is available from the British Library.

ISBN: 978-1-84680-812-8

Printed by Craft Print International Ltd., Singapore

Contents

Chapter 1 A holiday?.............................. 5

Chapter 2 Time to go.............................. 8

Chapter 3 So close 20

Chapter 4 The smell of freedom 25

Chapter 5 A deal is signed.................... 35

Characters

Marya

Emil

Pepik

Grey Coat

The teddy bear guard

Chapter 1
A holiday?

'We're going on a holiday tomorrow,' said Marya Burgan. Her son, Pepik, looked up from his homework.

'But what about school?' asked Pepik.

'You're going to have a holiday from school, too,' she said.

Pepik could hardly believe his ears. 'Where are we going?' he asked.

His mother didn't answer but Pepik didn't really care where they were going. 'Anywhere has to be better than here,' he thought.

Pepik's home town was no longer a good place to live. Not since the men in the long grey coats arrived. Children no longer played outside. They rushed home as soon as school finished. Pepik noticed that more and more of his classmates weren't even at school now. And being at home wasn't any better. There was no television and there never seemed to be enough to eat.

Pepik was sure that it all had to do with the men in the long grey coats. They were always coming to his house, looking for his father. Pepik's father, Emil, was a scientist who worked in a place surrounded by security guards. That was all that Pepik knew.

'This is no ordinary holiday,' thought Pepik as he packed his bag. He wondered if they were leaving for good. If they were, he knew it was because his parents had no choice. As he closed his bag, he let out a loud sigh. He felt nervous, but excited too. Whatever lay ahead of them had to be better than this misery.

Chapter 2
Time to go

The next morning was cold and damp.

In the night, Pepik had heard his parents packing the car. He crept down the stairs. He watched as his parents pulled the car apart, hiding papers in the roof lining. 'That's strange,' thought Pepik. 'But I bet I'm right – we are running away.

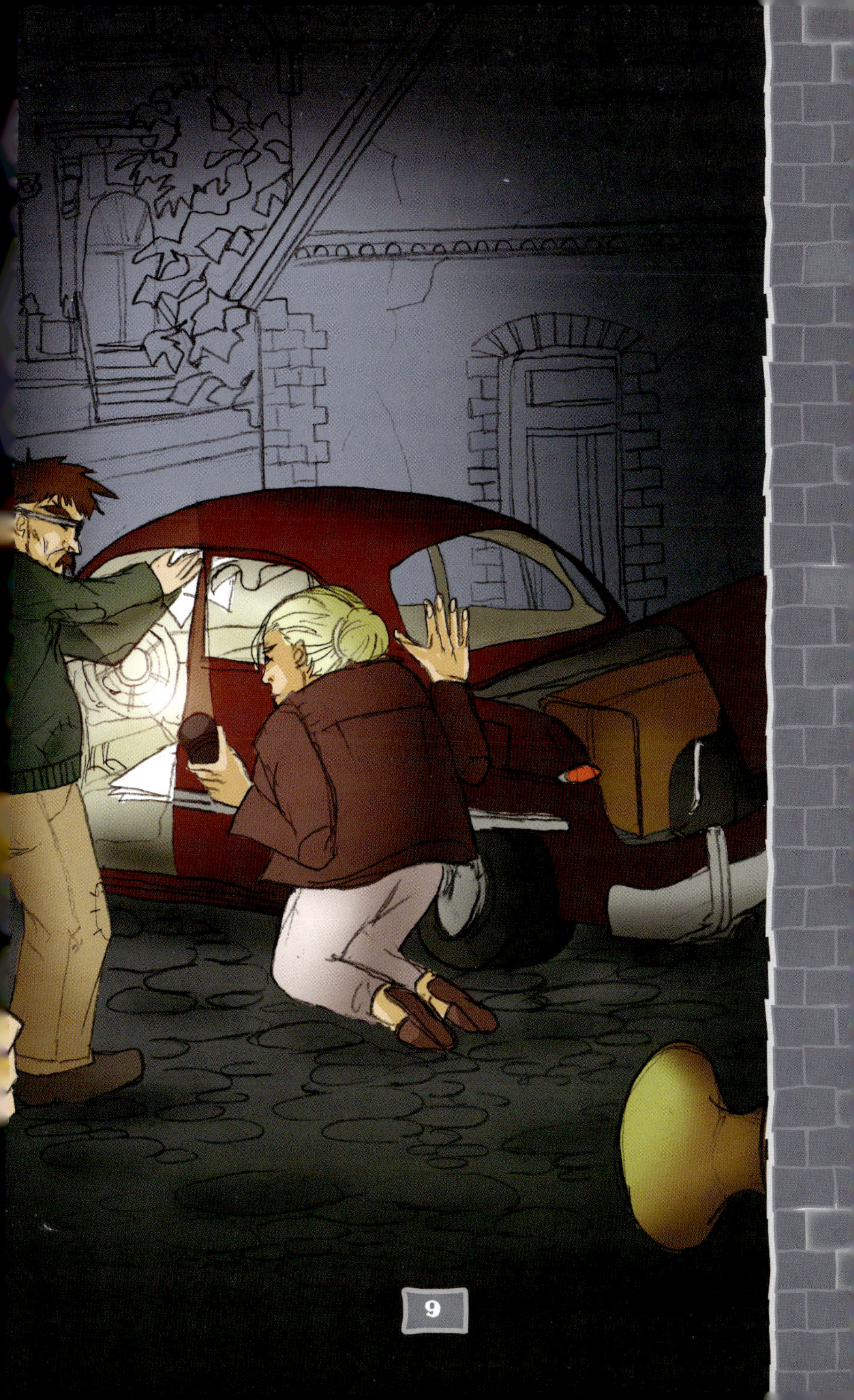

Finally, it was time to go. Marya pulled the door closed behind them, her hand lingering on the doorknob. Emil smiled at her. After a few moments, she let go of the door. Then the three of them got in the car and drove off.

The car trip was long, made even longer by the fact that no-one spoke. The only sound was the radio. Not music—news. Emil kept changing the station to get the best reception. Pepik didn't listen. He was too busy worrying about what lay ahead.

After what seemed like hours, they reached a long queue of cars.

'Where are we, Papa?' asked Pepik.

'This is the border, Pepik.'

'Why are all the cars lined up? It wasn't like this when we crossed the border before.'

Marya turned around and answered him. 'The border guards are checking the cars. Don't worry, Pepik,' she said. 'We're just going on a holiday. What could they possibly want with us?'

Pepik thought about the papers he had seen his parents hiding in the car. This was no holiday. The secret police wanted his father.

He began to panic. What if the border guards asked him questions about where they were going and what they were doing? He would have to lie. 'What will I say?' he thought. 'Will I give away too much?'

They neared the checkpoint. Marya held their documents ready for the border guards.

The queue inched forward. Finally, Pepik could see the checkpoint up ahead. Two uniformed guards operated the barrier.

On either side were small buildings where the border guards worked. All the guards had guns. More uniformed men walked along the line of cars. They looked into car windows, reading people's documents and talking on radios.

Pepik watched as the car ahead of them was pulled over. A man, a woman and a small girl got out. The border guard began pulling everything out of the car—bags, boxes, even the spare tyre. He dumped all the people's belongings into a great pile. The woman was sobbing on the man's shoulder. The girl clutched her mother's leg with one hand and held tightly to a teddy bear with the other.

Pepik could not take his eyes off them. Then the guard snatched the bear from the girl. He looked it over, then threw the teddy onto the ground. The little girl looked like she might cry.

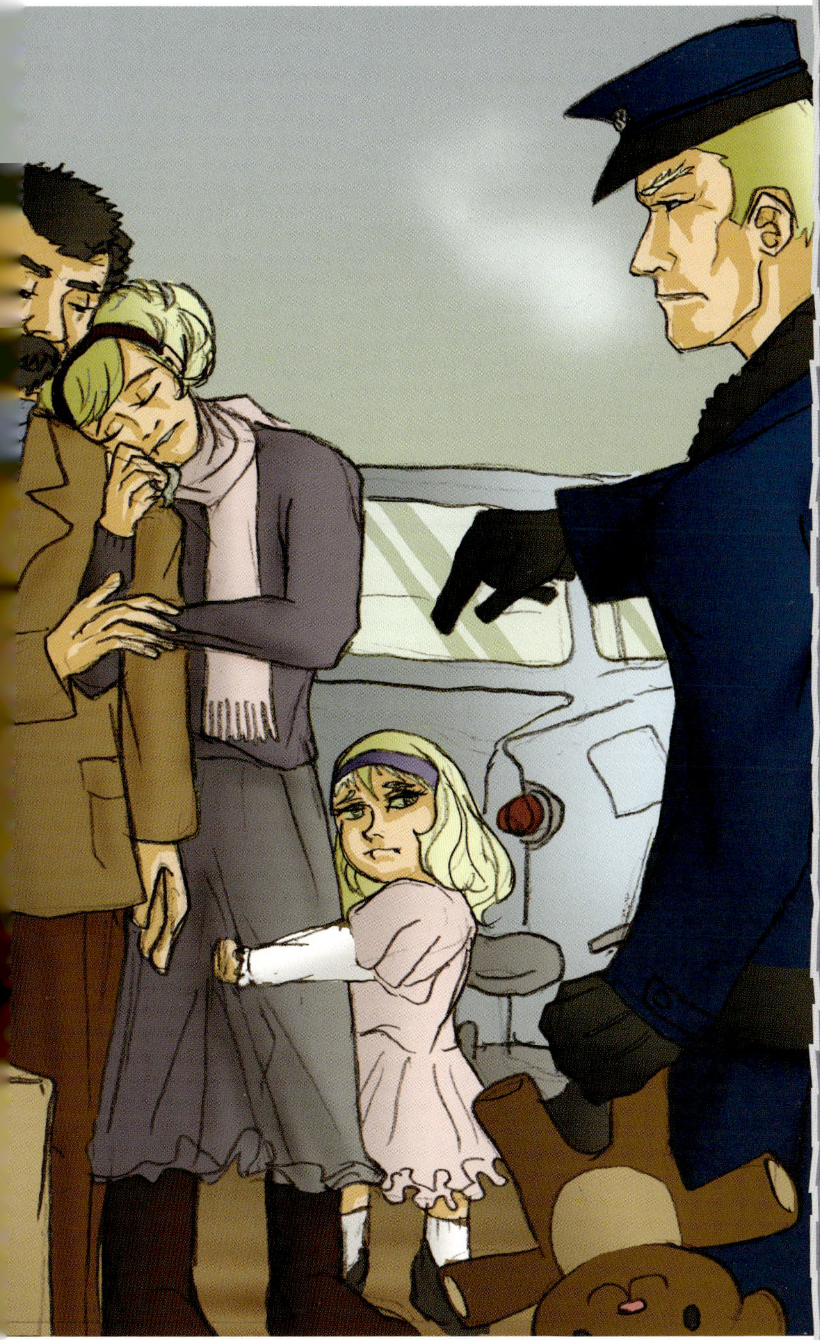

Something snapped inside Pepik. He flung open the door. His mother called after him. He could hear the terror in her voice but nothing would stop him.

He walked over to the teddy bear on the ground and picked it up. He gave it to the little girl. She looked up at him with a big smile.

Pepik felt warm inside, despite the cold day.

'You! You, boy!' Pepik froze as a hand grabbed his shoulder. He felt something cold, hard and metallic brush his hand. Only then did he realise how foolish he had been. His mouth went dry and his legs began to shake.

Pepik's mother ran up. 'I'm sorry, sir. So sorry, sir,' she said. 'He didn't mean to make trouble. Please forgive him.'

The guard gave him a shake, then let him go. 'Go back to your car,' he growled, 'and stay there.'

Pepik and his mother hurried back to the car. Pepik was confused about how he felt. Was he ashamed that his mother had to plead with this hateful man? Was he relieved to be free? Was he scared that now they would not be allowed across the border? He realised that he felt all those things. But mostly, he was angry.

In the car, Marya turned to him. Her look made him a little scared.

'Pepik, my son, I know you only did what you thought was right, but it wasn't! You have no idea …' She stopped as tears began to roll down her cheek.

His father spoke quietly. 'Pepik, you're a good boy. Helping that little girl was brave. But what good is bravery if they take you away?'

Pepik sat down in his seat. He was thinking about what his father had said when he realised he had an answer to his father's question. Quietly to himself, he said, 'At least then they won't take you.'

Chapter 3
So close

There were now only two cars ahead of them at the checkpoint. So far, none of the border guards had come near their car. Was this their lucky day? But just as Pepik began to relax, one of the guards stuck his hand in their window and ordered, 'Documents please!' He grabbed the papers from Pepik's mother and began looking them over.

Pepik watched his parents. His mother was taking deep breaths. His father's hands were tight on the steering wheel, and his knuckles were white.

'Where are you going?' asked the guard. Emil said that they were going on a short holiday.

The guard didn't take his eyes off their documents. 'Open the boot, please.'

Emil got out and opened the boot. Pepik turned around in his seat, trying to see what was happening. 'Pepik, sit down!' said his mother. She spoke quietly but Pepik could hear the fear in her voice. He sat down.

Pepik heard the boot close. His father walked to the front of the car. The guard gave back their documents.

'Thank you, Mr Burgan,' said the guard. 'Remember to keep to your plan and return on the day you intend. Or, there may be trouble.'

Pepik held his breath until his father was back in the car. He sighed with relief. Everything was going to be OK. Now they had only to wait for the cars in front of them to move and they could be on their way.

It was a terrible wait. What was taking so long? Finally, the front car drove off.

Relieved, Pepik flopped back in his seat. He could see the tension lift from his parents' shoulders.

'Only one more car to go and we're free,' he said to himself.

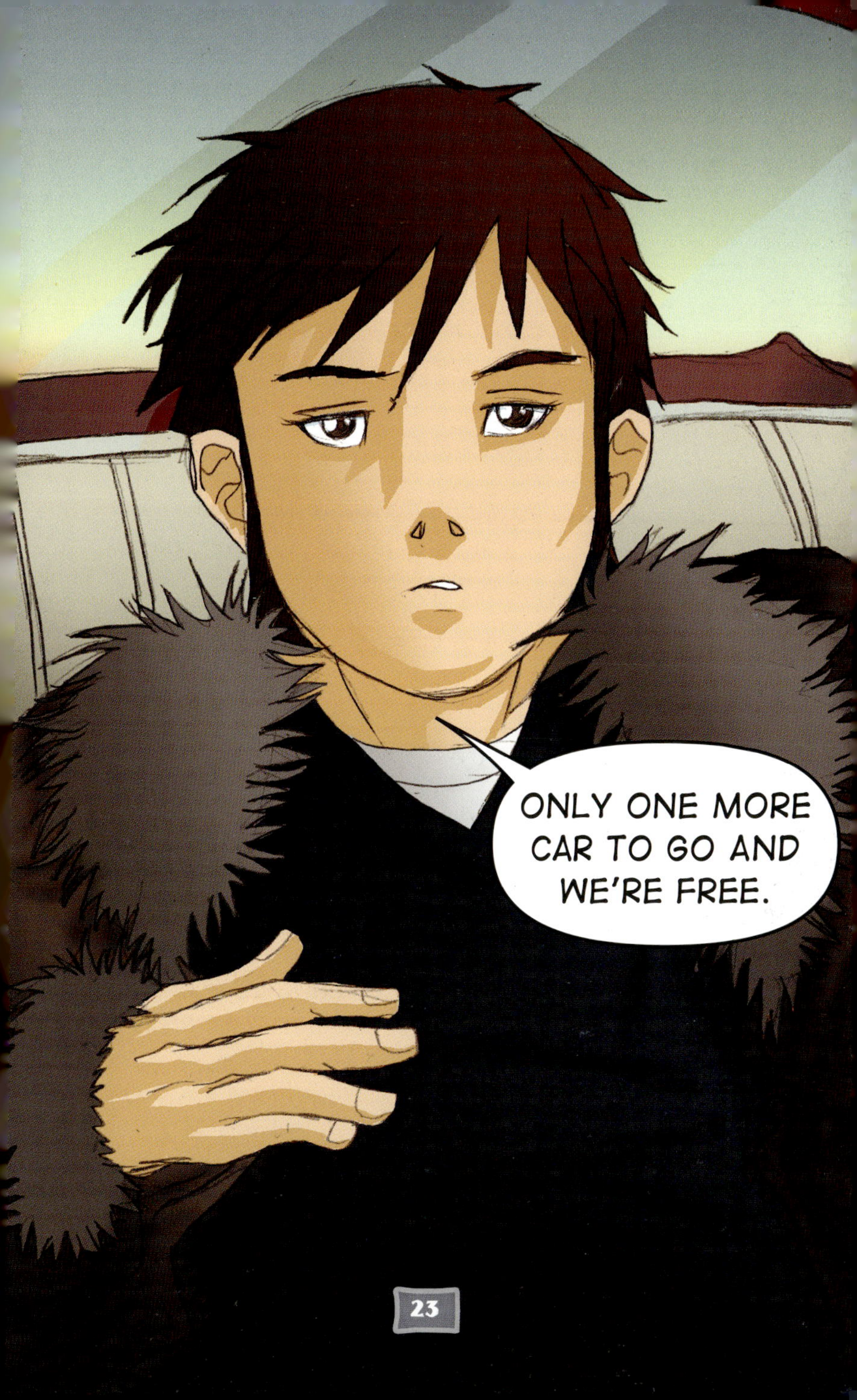
ONLY ONE MORE CAR TO GO AND WE'RE FREE.

They were now alongside the guards' buildings. Pepik tried to see inside the tinted windows. He couldn't see a thing. A guard was controlling the barrier.

They waited, but the car in front didn't budge.

'Why aren't we going, Papa?'

'Sssh now, Pepik. We'll be on our way soon.' All three were staring at the car in front when it happened.

Tap, tap, tap. Someone was knocking on their window. But it was not a border control guard. It was a man in a long grey coat. They had been found out!

Chapter 4
The smell of freedom

Emil opened the window.

'Come with me, Mr Burgan,' ordered Grey Coat. Pepik wanted to grab hold of his father. He wanted to tell Grey Coat to go away, to leave his family alone. But he knew he couldn't. Instead, he watched helplessly.

His father turned to Pepik and Marya. He smiled and nodded as if to say that everything would be all right. But there was fear in his eyes. Pepik felt sick in his stomach.

'Be still, Pepik,' his mother said. 'Your father will be back soon.' But Pepik could see tears in her eyes.

Pepik watched Grey Coat take his father into the guards' building. What would happen to him? Would they lock him up? Or perhaps something even worse?

The barrier was raised and the car in front of them drove off. Two guards with even bigger guns moved to stand in front of the Burgans' car.

Pepik and his mother waited and waited. Pepik turned around and saw the long line of cars waiting behind them, waiting for their chance of freedom. Perhaps this was a good sign, he thought. If anything really bad was going to happen, the guards would have moved their car off to one of those little parking bays. They would be letting the other cars through. Wouldn't they?

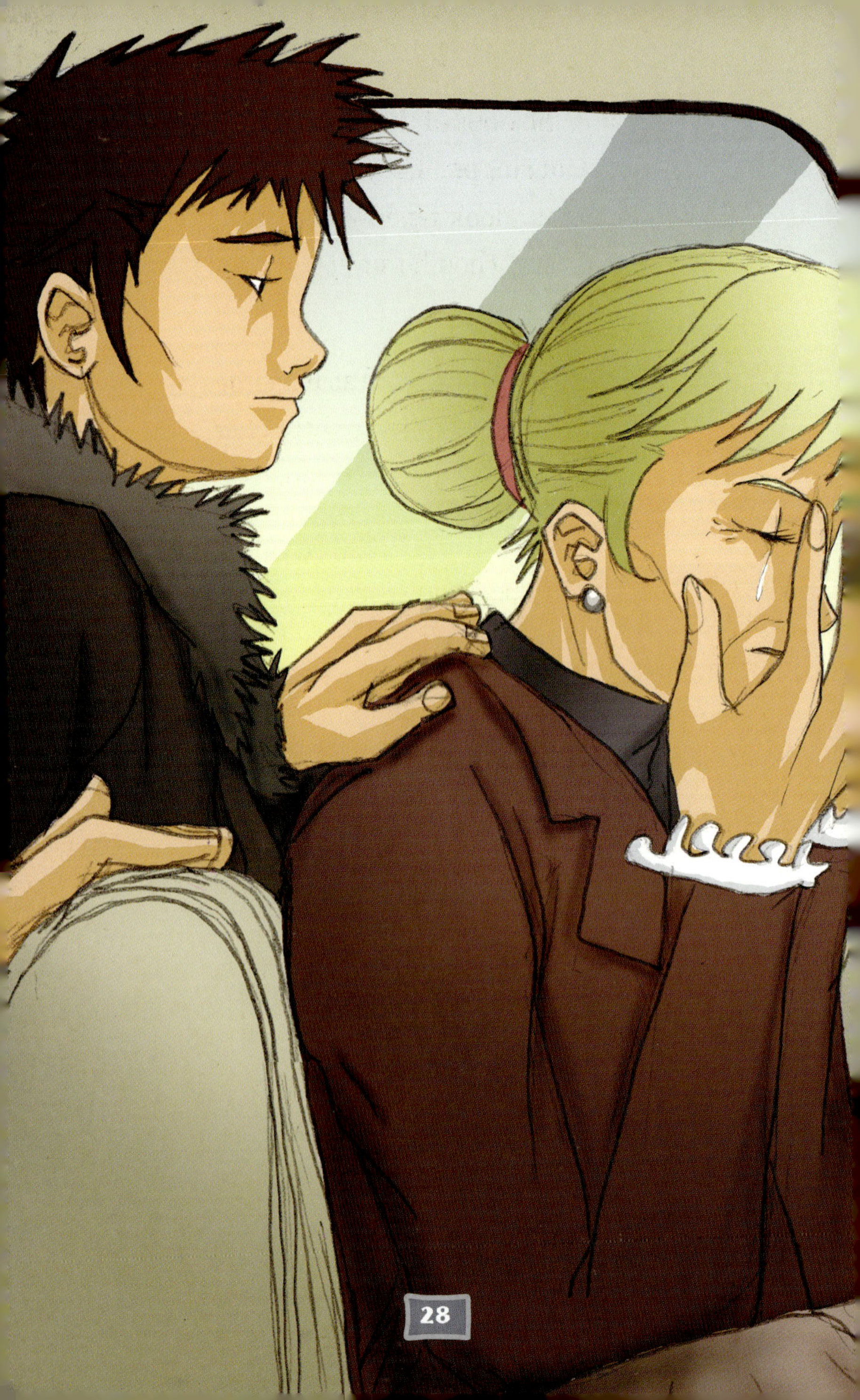

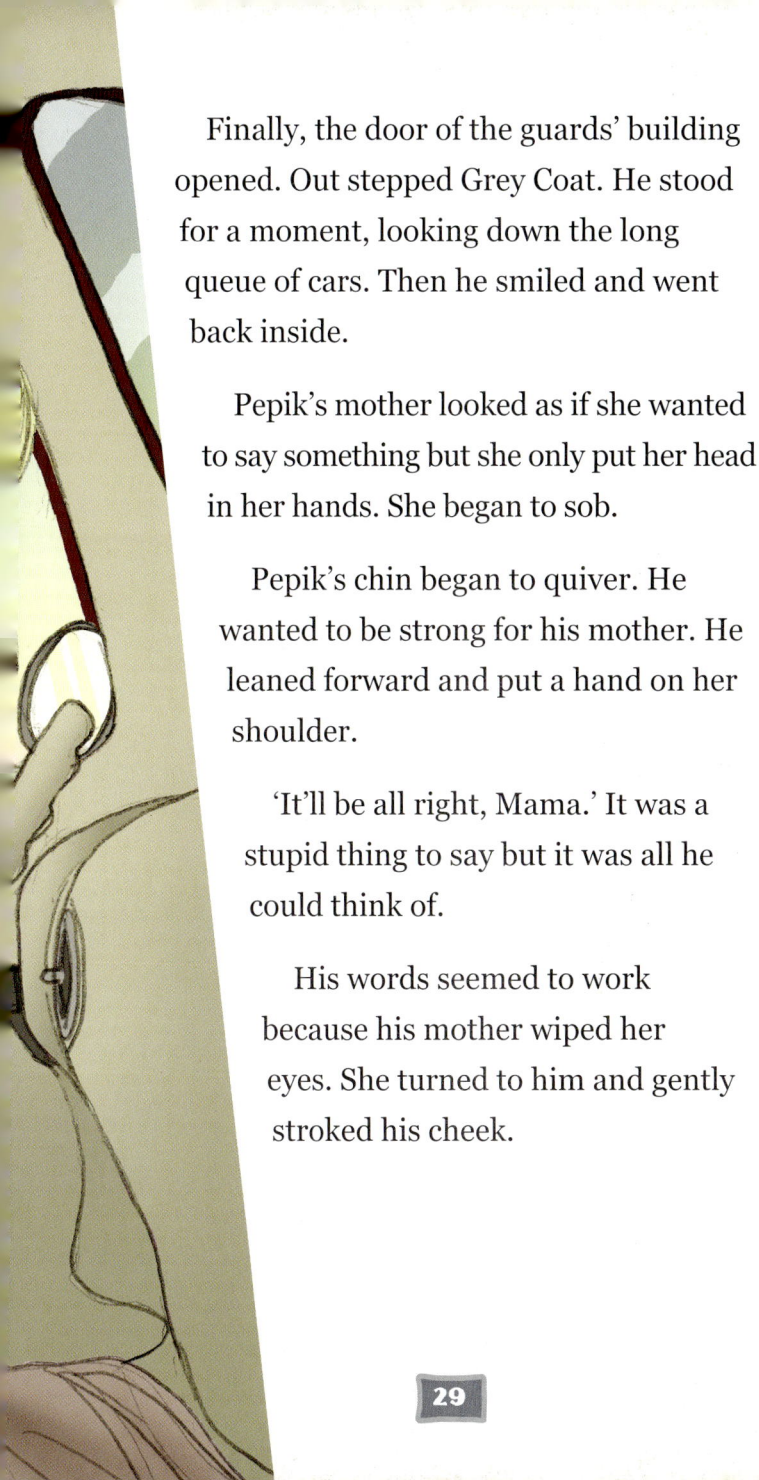

Finally, the door of the guards' building opened. Out stepped Grey Coat. He stood for a moment, looking down the long queue of cars. Then he smiled and went back inside.

Pepik's mother looked as if she wanted to say something but she only put her head in her hands. She began to sob.

Pepik's chin began to quiver. He wanted to be strong for his mother. He leaned forward and put a hand on her shoulder.

'It'll be all right, Mama.' It was a stupid thing to say but it was all he could think of.

His words seemed to work because his mother wiped her eyes. She turned to him and gently stroked his cheek.

With that, Pepik quickly leaned forward and kissed his mother on the cheek. 'I love you, Mama,' he said. Then he jumped out of the car.

'Pepik, no! Not again!' his mother screamed. But Pepik was determined to do something, anything, to save his father.

He went up to the guards' building and banged on the door.

'Take *me*! Take *me*!' he screamed. 'Leave my father alone! He didn't take the teddy bear! I did! It was me!' Pepik knew that this wasn't the reason they had taken his father. He hoped that maybe, just maybe, Grey Coat would let Emil go in exchange for him. Anything was worth a try to save his father.

LEAVE MY FATHER ALONE!

Finally, the door opened. Pepik fell back. He saw a pair of polished, black boots. He looked up. It was Grey Coat.

The man kicked him aside like dirt. As Pepik got up off the ground, he saw his father come through the door. His father looked at him with surprise and fear but didn't say a word.

Grey Coat led them towards their car and opened the door for Pepik. Quickly, he climbed inside and the man closed the door.

'Stop! Stop!' called a voice. Pepik looked around to see who it was. His heart seemed to stop beating. It was the border guard from before, the teddy bear guard!

Chapter 5
A deal is signed

The teddy bear guard, Grey Coat and Emil were now talking together. Pepik could not hear what they were saying. They looked at him all the time. Grey Coat went back inside the building and returned a moment later with a piece of paper. He pushed a pen into Pepik's father's hand. Emil thought for a moment, then signed the paper.

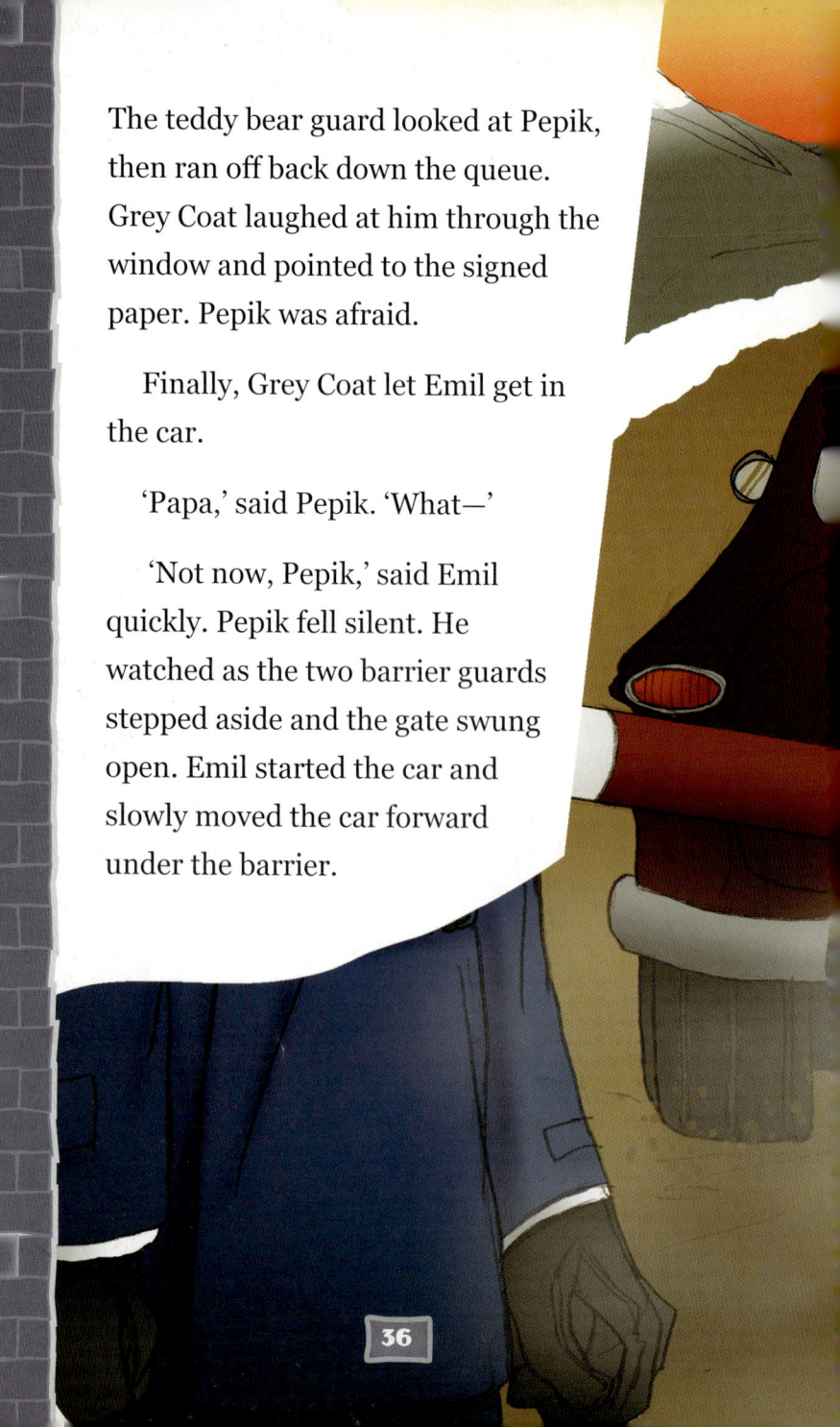

The teddy bear guard looked at Pepik, then ran off back down the queue. Grey Coat laughed at him through the window and pointed to the signed paper. Pepik was afraid.

Finally, Grey Coat let Emil get in the car.

'Papa,' said Pepik. 'What—'

'Not now, Pepik,' said Emil quickly. Pepik fell silent. He watched as the two barrier guards stepped aside and the gate swung open. Emil started the car and slowly moved the car forward under the barrier.

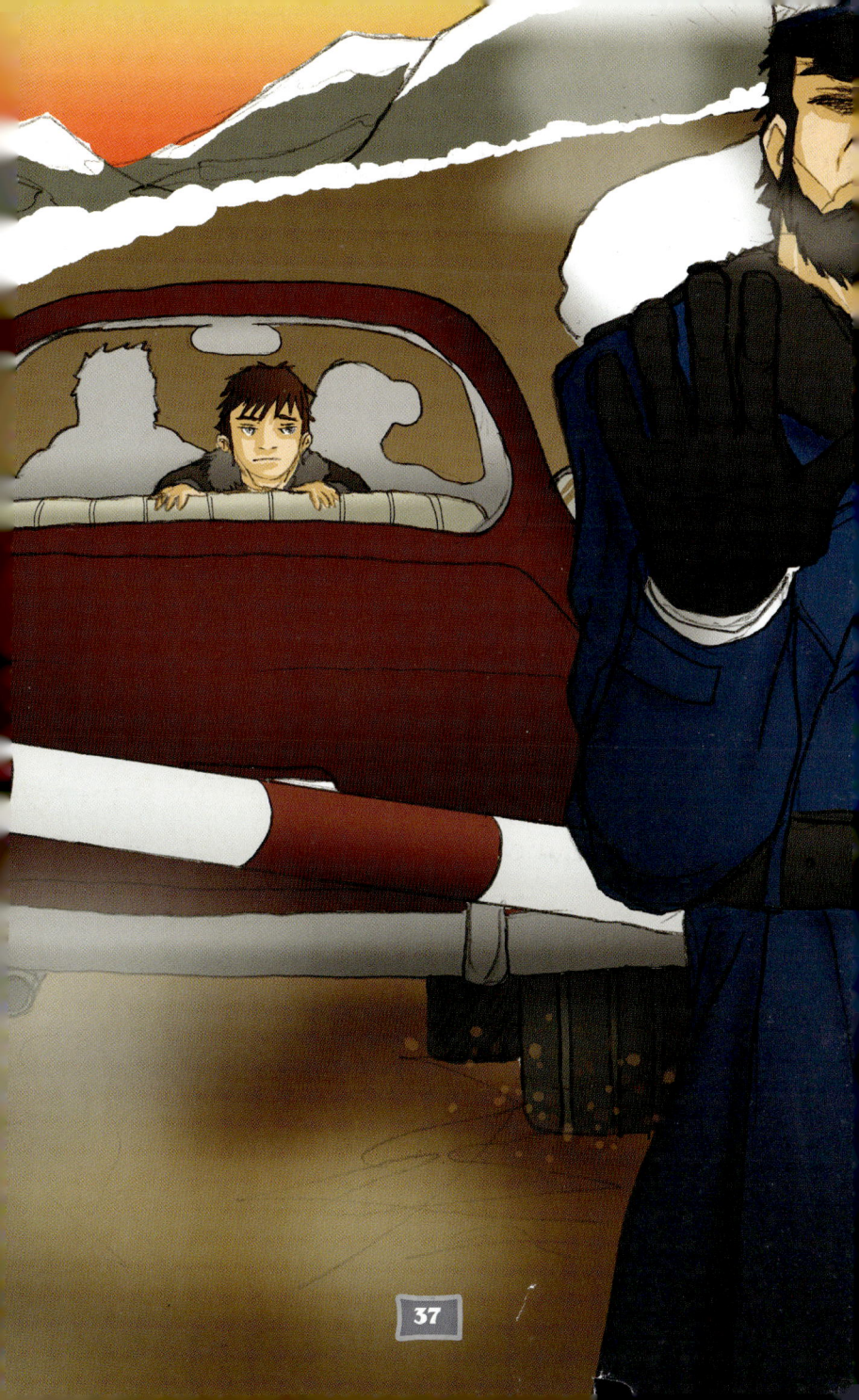

They drove in silence. After what felt like hours, his father pulled the car over to the side of the road. He turned to Pepik.

'Pepik,' he began.

'I know, Papa,' said Pepik. 'I know we're not going on a holiday. I saw you hiding documents in the car last night. The secret police want you, don't they? We're leaving for good.'

'Oh Pepik, I'm sorry,' sighed Emil. 'I had no idea you knew. Your mother and I thought it best not to tell you what was happening. We were trying to protect you.' He smiled at his wife. 'Our son is much braver than we thought.'

'But Emil, what was that paper that you signed?' asked Marya.

Emil was silent for a moment. Then he spoke. 'To have our freedom, I had to make a deal. I signed an agreement for Pepik to go to the national training camp when we return from our holiday.'

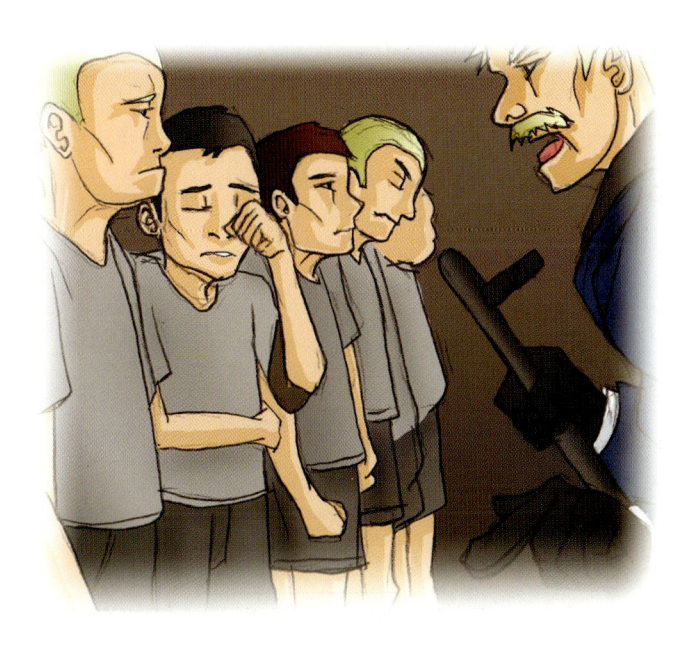

Marya gasped. Pepik's jaw dropped. He had heard of these camps. None of the boys who went there ever returned.

'You see,' his father went on, 'they were about to check our car. That's why I was coming out—to move the car. But then that guard came running up. He wanted to report you for helping that little girl with the teddy bear. He said you were a trouble-maker. The man in the grey coat got distracted by that and forgot about searching the car.'

Emil stopped for a moment, then went on. 'They could have found the papers, Pepik,' he said. 'Our escape plan would have been discovered. But your brave act with that little girl and her teddy bear ended up saving us! I'm so proud of you!'

'But what about the camp?' asked Pepik.

'Don't worry, Pepik. We will never return here for them to take you. Now we are free! We shall not live in fear again, I promise you both.'

Pepik finally relaxed. He leaned forward and hugged his parents. No matter where they went next, they were free.